D0679907

To Suzanne, Ginny and Mikey

SPANISH SLANGUAGE

SPANISH SLANGUAGE

A *FUN* VISUAL GUIDE TO SPANISH TERMS AND PHRASES BY MIKE ELLIS

First Edition
14 13   8 9 10 11

Text © 2010 Mike Ellis
Illustrations © 2010 Rupert Bottenberg
except vectorstock.com

All rights reserved. No part of this book may be
reproduced by any means whatsoever without
written permission from the publisher, except brief
portions quoted for purpose of review.

Published by
Gibbs Smith
P.O. Box 667
Layton, Utah 84041

1.800.835.4993 orders
www.gibbs-smith.com

Designed by Michel Vrana
Printed and bound in Hong Kong

Gibbs Smith books are printed on paper produced
from sustainable PEFC-certified forest/controlled
wood source.
Learn more at: www.pefc.org

Library of Congress Cataloging-in-Publication Data

Ellis, Mike, 1961-
  Spanish slanguage : a fun visual guide to Spanish
terms and phrases / Mike Ellis. — 1st ed.
     p. cm.
  ISBN-13: 978-1-4236-0749-6
  ISBN-10: 1-4236-0749-X
  1. Spanish language—Conversation and phrase
books—English. I. Title.
  PC4121.E625 2010
  468.2'421—dc22
                                    2009032975

CONTENTS

I'd like to acknowledge all the folks at Gibbs Smith who were open-minded enough to take on a project like this.

And to my mom who instilled in me an appreciation for listening. My ability to listen has enabled me to teach anybody a new language using the language skills they already possess.

HOW TO USE THIS BOOK

If you have always wanted to learn the basics of Spanish, but traditional methods seemed overwhelming or tedious, this book is for you! Just follow the directions below and soon you'll be able to say dozens of Spanish words and phrases.

• Follow the illustrated prompts and say the phrase quickly and smoothly with emphasis on the word highlighted with the red starburst.

• Learn to string together phrases so you can create many more phrases.

• Add "no" to the front or back of a phrase or make the phrase a question by inflecting your voice.

• Draw your own pictures to help with memorization and pronunciation.

Note: This book may produce Americanized Spanish.

For free sound bytes, visit slanguage.com

GREETINGS AND RESPONSES

How's it going?
¿Cómo va?

 **Comb Oh Vah?**

Fine, and yourself?
Bien, ¿y tú?

 **Bee Any 2?**

What's happening?
¿Qué pasa?

Kay Pasta?

Fine
Bien

Very well
Muy bien

Stupendous
Estupendo

With pleasure
Con gusto

Cone Goose Toe

My pleasure
Me gusto

May Goose Toe

Welcome
Bienvenido

Bee Yen Ven Knee Doe

Thank you
Gracias

Grassy Us

Yes, yes, yes
Sí, sí, sí

See See See

No, no, no
No, no, no

No No No

I must / I need
Yo necesito

 **Joe Nay Say See Toe**

What do you say?
¿Qué dice?

 **Kay Dee Say?**

Not much, yourself?
No mucho, ¿tú?

 **No Mooch Oh 2 ?**

What's new?
¿Qué hay de nuevo?

Kay Eye Day New Wave Oh?

Very, very, very
Muy, muy, muy

Moo We Moo We Moo We

In a moment
Momentito

Moment Tee Toe

A little bit
Poquito

Poe Key Toe

With me?
¿Conmigo?

Cone Me Go?

With me, my friends?
¿Conmigo mis amigos?

Cone Me Go Meese a Me Goes?

Can we?
¿Podemos?

Poe Dame Owes?

Yes
Sí

See

That's great
Qué bien

Kay Bee Yen

I know
Yo se

Joe Say

I don't know
Yo no se

ADJECTIVES

Beautiful
Bello

Bay Yo

Handsome
Lindo

Lean Doe

Happy
Contento

Cone 10 Toe

24 ADJECTIVES

Comfortable
Cómodo

Smooth
Liso

Solid
Sólido

Stupendous
Estupendo

Ace 2 Pen Doe

Subtle
Sutil

Sue Teal

Pretty
Bonito

Bow Knee Toe

FAMILY

Mother
Madre

Mod Ray

Father
Padre

Pod Ray

Brother
Hermano

Air Ma Know

Sister
Hermana

Air Ma Na

Aunt
Tía

Tee a

Uncle
Tío

Tee Oh

Daughter
Hija

Ee Hah

Son
Hijo

Ee Hoe

Grandmother
Abuela

Obb Way La

Grandfather
Abuelo

Obb Way Low

Granddaughter
Nieta

Knee Yet a

Grandson
Nieto

Knee Yet Toe

Husband
Esposo

Wife
Esposa

QUESTIONS

What?
¿Qué?

Kay?

Where?
¿Dónde?

Done Day?

Why?
¿Por qué?

Pour Kay?

Why not?
¿Cómo no?

Comb **Oh No?**

Who?
¿Quién?

Key Yen ?

Is it?
¿Es?

A ♠

Ace?

Are there?
¿Hay?

Eye?

How do you say?
¿Cómo se dice?

Comb Oh Say Dee Say?

How?
¿Cómo?

Comb Oh?

40 QUESTIONS

What's this mean?
¿Qué significa?

Kay See Knee Fee Kah?

Where do you live?
¿Dónde vive?

Done Day Vee Vay?

Whose is this?
¿De quien es?

Day Key Yen Ace?

Also?
¿También?

Tom Bee Yen?

With you?
¿Contigo?

Cone Tee Go?

Here?
¿Aquí?

A Key?

Not here?
¿No aquí?

Noah Key?

Can you?
¿Puede?

P'Way Day?

Do you have . . . ?
¿Tiene . . . ?

Tee Any...?

Do you have it?
¿Tiénelo?

Tee Any Low?

What do you want?
¿Qué quiere?

Kay Key Eddie?

Your address?
¿Su dirección?

Sue Deed Ex See Own?

FOOD AND RESTAURANTS

I'm drinking it
Yo lo bebo

I'm eating it
Yo lo como

I like it
Me gusta

I'm enjoying it
Yo lo gozo

I'm thirsty
Tengo sed

I'd like
Yo quiero

Do you have?
¿Tú tienes?

2 Tee Yen Ace?

Delicious
Gustoso

Goose Toe So

With cheese
Con queso

Cone Kay So

With lemon
Con limón

 Cone Lee Moan

Bacon
Tocino

 Toe See No

Chicken
Pollo

 Poe Yo

Beef
Carne

Car Neigh

Octopus
Pulpitos

Pool Pea Toes

Sweet Potato
El boniato

Elbow Knee Yacht Toe

Shrimp
Camarón

Come Odd Own

Tuna
Atún

Ah Tune

Asparagus
Espárragos

Ace Pod Ah Goes

Pepper
Pimiento

Pea Me Yen Toe

Rice
Arroz

Add Owes

Beans
Frijoles

Free Hole Ace

Drinks
Bebidas

Water
Agua

Wine
Vino

LABOR

Bolt
Perno

Pear No

Bucket
Balde

Ball Day

Cement
Cemento

Say Main Toe

Equipment
Equipo

Ache Key Poe

Estimate
Estimación

Ace Tee Ma See Own

Floor
Piso

Pea So

Hacksaw
Sierra de amero

See Aid a Day a Maid a

Inch
Pulgada

Pool Gotta

Ladder
Escalera

Ace Call Aid a

Machinist
Mecánico

May **Connie** Co.

Metal
Metálico

May **Tolly** Co.

Method
Método

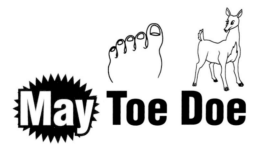

May Toe Doe

Meticulous
Meticuloso

May Tee Cool Oh So

Minimal
Mínimo

Me Knee Moe

Paintbrush
Brocha

Broach a

Smooth
Liso

Solid
Sólido

Thousand
Mil

Meal

Thousandth
Milésimo

 **Me Lay See Moe**

Tall/High
Alto

 **All Toe**

Weight
Peso

 **Pay So**

LAW ENFORCEMENT

Stop
Alto

All Toe

Police
Policía

Poe Lee See Ya

Stop! Police!
¡Alto! ¡Policía!

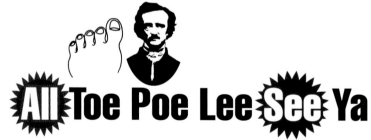
All Toe Poe Lee See Ya

I'm a police officer
Soy policía

Soy Poe Lee See Ya

Freeze
Quieto

Key Ate Toe

Everybody freeze
Todos quietos

Toe Dose Key Ate Toes

Don't move
No se mueve

Stay here
Quédese aquí

Look at me
Míreme

Slowly
Despacio

Calm down
Cálmese

Give it to me
Démelo

Silence
Silencio

See Lane See Oh

Don't touch me
No me toque

No May Toe Kay

Your address
Su dirección

Sue Deed Ex See Own

Agent
Agente

A Hen Tay

Citizen
Ciudadano

See You Dud Don Oh

Do you have it?
¿Tiénelo?

Tee Any Low?

Emergency
Emergencia

 Aim Mare Hen Seeya

Fight
Pelea

 Pay Lay a

Help
Ayuda

 Eye You'd a

Help me
Ayúdame

Eye You'd a May

I don't understand
No entiendo

No Wayne Tee Yen Doe

Injured?
¿Lastimado?

Loss Tee Mod Oh?

Is this yours?
¿Es suyo?

Ace Sue Yo?

Knowledge
Conocimiento

Cone Oh See Me Yen Toe

Lawyer
Abogado

A Bow God Oh

Liar
Mentiroso

Main Tee'd Oh So

License plate
Placa

P'lock a

Moment
Momento

Moe Main Toe

Murderer
Asesino

A Say Seen Oh

Obey me
Obedéceme

Obey Day Say May

Robbery
Robo

Roe Bow

Weapon
Arma

HEALTH AND MEDICINE

How's it going?
¿Cómo va?

Fine?
¿Bien?

Not well?
¿No bien?

Bump
Topetón

Toe Pay Tone

Comfortable
Cómodo

Comb Oh Doe

Earache
Dolor de oído

Dole Or Day Oh We Doe

Eardrum
Tímpano

Emphysema
Enfisema

Equipment
Equipo

Eyeball
Globo del ojo

Glow Bow Del Oh Hoe

Gentle
Suave

Swa Vay

Heart
Corazón

Code a Zone

Infection
Infección

In Feck See Own

Mumps
Paperas

Pop Paid Us

Muscle
Músculo

Moose Cool Oh

Nearsighted
Miope

Me Oh Pay

Nose
Nariz

Nod Ease

Nurse
Enfermara

An Fair Maid a

Oxygen
Oxígeno

Oak See Hen Oh

Pain
Dolor

Dole Or

Painful
Doloroso

Dole Ode Oh So

Painless
Sin dolor

Seen Dole Or

Peroxide
Peróxido

Paid Oak See Doe

Parasite
Parásito

Pod Ah See Toe

Physical
Físico

Physician
Médico

Sleep
Sueño

Throb
Latido

Lot Tee Doe

Tonsillitis
Tonsilitis

Tone See Lee Tease

TRAVEL AND TOURISM

Hotel
Hotel

Oh Tell

Airport
Aeropuerto

Eye Rope Where Toe

Cab or Taxi
Taxi

Tock See

Bus
Autobús

Ow Toe **Booze**

Ticket
Boleto

Bow **Lay** Toe

Restaurant
Restaurante

Rest Are **Ron** Tay

Bank
Banco

Restroom
Baño